A Glossary of SANSKRIT From the Spiritual Tradition of India

Diana Morrison

Nilgiri Press

Designed, printed, and bound by Nilgiri Press
Fifth printing April, 1984
ISBN *0–915132–12–5*

The Blue Mountain Center of Meditation, founded in Berkeley in 1960 by Eknath Easwaran, publishes books on how to lead the spiritual life in the home and the community. Please write for information to Nilgiri Press, Box 477, Petaluma, California 94953.

Introduction

Almost since the beginning of recorded history in India, Sanskrit has been the religious and literary language of Hinduism. To trace the long history of Sanskrit, we must go back in time to about 2500 years before the birth of Christ. It was between four and five thousand years ago that Sanskrit appeared in the sacred literature of the nomadic tribes which were slowly migrating into India through the passes and valleys of the Punjab, "the Land of Five Rivers," on the northwest frontier of India. There, on the upper reaches of the Indus River, the earliest hymns of the Rig Veda were sung, invoking the blessings of the many powerful and beautiful gods and goddesses of the natural world.

Actually, the history of Sanskrit reaches even further back, into the "dark backward and abysm of time." The research of modern scholars has revealed that Sanskrit is a child of a forgotten language, Indo-European, which was used by the ancestors of modern speakers of Indo-European languages. Thus, Sanskrit is the eastern cousin of Latin, Greek, English, French, Spanish, and many other European languages. We date Sanskrit from the time when the eastward migrating Indo-Europeans reached the frontier of India, sometime before 2000 B.C. When the āryans–'noble people,' as they called themselves–reached India and confronted the highly developed native Dravidian culture, the fertile union of these two peoples gave birth to the rich and long-lived Hindu tradition.

Since that time there has been a continuous religious and cultural tradition in India, despite much disturbing political disunity and the challenge of various foreign invasions. This strong tradition has been preserved for the most part in the Sanskrit language, and we inherit substantial Sanskrit documents from each period of Indian history. From the Vedic Age we have the powerful hymns of the Samhitā, as well as the priestly commentaries of the Brāhmanas and Āranyakas—and, most important, the writings of the mystics, the Upanishads. As the center of Sanskrit culture moved from the mountainous frontier down onto the fertile plain of the river Ganges, royal cities were established and the Epic Age began. Over many centuries, beginning in the first millennium B.C., the great epic the *Mahābhārata* was composed, compiled, and passed from singer to singer and from generation to generation, recounting the heroic lives of the five Pāndava princes, and inspiring all listeners with devotion for God in his miraculous and mighty form as Sri Krishna. From the Epic Age we also have the story of another great incarnation called Rāma: the *Rāmāyana,* which tells the story of the cosmic battle between good and evil.

Then, as Indian society settled down into sophisticated cities along the banks of the Ganges and southwards, the refined Classical Age began, the age of the secular poets who still remembered and retold the old tales of gods and saints, but who rejoiced in the beauty of human love and the world of nature. From the many masterpieces of this age, the Indian critics always point out Kālidāsa's *Shakuntalā* as the drama beyond comparison. Later, in the Medieval period, we have Jayadeva's *Gītagovinda,* retelling the story of Krishna's love in lyrical Sanskrit. From the great religious renewal of the medieval times we have many hymns to Shiva, Vishnu, and the Divine Mother, both in Sanskrit and in the everyday languages of the people.

This is just a part of what has been left to us of the great Sanskritic tradition. Even today these epic stories, plays, and hymns communicate a profound message to Hindu India, where ordinary people still look upon Sanskrit as the language of the gods and hold even the sounds of its alphabet sacred. Outside India, Sanskrit is valued everywhere for its sophisticated and precise grammar and for its depth of philosophic insight.

The purpose of this glossary is to provide brief, precise definitions to the words of central importance to India's spiritual teachings. Because it has been the language of a society that places the highest value on religious experience and practice, Sanskrit possesses many precise terms for spiritual concepts and disciplines. These precise terms often resist translation, and even a brief acquaintance with a basic Sanskrit vocabulary can help in appreciating mystical texts such as the Bhagavad Gīta. For example, the word *sādhana* (literally 'that which leads straight to the goal') refers to a program of disciplines such as meditation, sense-control, etc. which leads to the goal of Self-realization. There is really no English word which can translate the full meaning of the word *sādhana*. It is for lack of an English equiva-that many Sanskrit words have been borrowed into English and are now used as practically everyday vocabulary: words like *yoga, karma, guru, mantram,* and even *kundalinī.*

Etymologies are sometimes included in the glossary where they are of particular interest. The word *Sanskrit* literally means 'perfected,' 'polished,' and it is a sophisticated language, based upon a complex system of roots and derivations. The entire Sanskrit language, including root lists and derivations, was described in amazing detail during the fourth century B.C. by the Indian grammatical genius Pānini, who demonstrated that the majority of Sanskrit words can be derived from a fixed number of roots. For example, the root syllable *kṛ* 'to do,' 'to make' underlies the verb *karoti* 'he makes,' and numerous related nouns such as *karma* 'action,' *kārya* 'a task to be done,' *kartṛ* 'doer,' and the suffix *-kāra* 'maker' as in the word *ahamkāra* 'I-maker,' 'that which makes me I.' Thus the study of Sanskrit etymology helps to throw light on the concepts behind much of its philosophical and mystical terminology.

But though Sanskrit is a refined and literary language, it is also capable of communicating in a direct, practical manner the important facts of the spiritual life. Not only poets but the most practical saints have been devoted to Sanskrit. The Upanishads often convey metaphysical teachings with a simple, earthy image. Even Mahatma Gandhi, who was so devoted to solving the most immediate down-to-earth problems, studied Sanskrit while in prison. Sanskrit is of use to everyone interested in the spiritual life, and of course to all students of Indian culture.

Sanskrit Alphabet and System of English Transliteration

Vowels

Simple

अ a आ ā इ i ई ī उ u ऊ ū ऋ ṛi ॠ ṛī ऌ ḷi

Diphthongs ए e ऐ ai ओ o औ au

When joined with a consonant the vowel characters are modified. For example, with the consonant क k, the vowels look like this:

ka	kā	ki	kī	ku	kū	kṛi	kṛī	kḷi	ke	kai	ko	kau
क	का	कि	की	कु	कू	कृ	कॄ	कॢ	के	कै	को	कौ

Consonants

guttural	क k	ख kh	ग g	घ gh	ङ ñ		
palatal	च ch	छ chh	ज j	झ jh	ञ ñ	य y	श ś
retroflex	ट ṭ	ठ ṭh	ड ḍ	ढ ḍh	ण ṇ	र r	ष sh
dental	त t	थ th	द d	ध dh	न n	ल l	स s
labial	प p	फ ph	ब b	भ bh	म m	व v	

aspiration ह h anusvāra ं ṃ visarga ः ḥ

Guide to Pronunciation

Vowels. Every Sanskrit vowel (except लृ ḷi) has two forms – a short and a long. The long form is pronounced twice as long as the short. In the English transliteration the long vowels are marked with a bar (-). The diphthongs are also pronounced twice as long as the short vowels. Thus in the words नील *nī · la* "blue" or गोप *go · pa* "cowherd," the first syllable is held twice as long as the second

a as in	*u*p
ā	f*a*ther
i	g*i*ve
ī	s*ee*
u	p*u*t
ū	r*u*le
ṛi	wr*i*tten
ṛī	wr*i*tten (but held twice as long)
ḷi	ab*le*
e	th*ey*
ai	*ai*sle
o	g*o*
au	c*ow*

Consonants. Consonants are generally pronounced as in English, but there are some differences. Sanskrit has many so called "aspirated consonants, that is, consonants pronounced with a slight *h* sound. For example, the consonant फ *ph* is pronounced as English *p* followed by an *h* as in ha*ph*azard. The भ *bh* is as in a*bh*or. The aspirated consonants are ख घ छ झ ठ ढ थ ध फ भ
kh gh chh jh ṭh ḍh th dh ph bh.

Note also the series of retroflex consonants ट ठ ड ढ ण ष
ṭ ṭh ḍ ḍh ṇ sh. Though pronounced almost like the English equivalents, they differ in being pronounced with the tip of the tongue

bent back and touching the roof of the mouth. The retroflex ष *sh* is somewhat like the English ru*ss*ian.

ch as in	*ch*urch
ñ	ca*ny*on
ṅ	si*ng*
ṃ	*m*an
h	*h*ome
g	*g*old
j	*J*une
ś	*sh*ip
ḥ	is a slight *h*

The other consonants are as in English.

A few words should be said about the format. Though the diacritical marks such as the accents, dots, lines and so on, may seem strange in the beginning, they are necessary if the English spelling of the Sanskrit word is to convey something of the original pronunciation.

Etymologies are included in square brackets.

The alphabetical order is not that used in English dictionaries, but that used in standard Sanskrit dictionaries, as follows:

a ā i ī u ū ṛi ṛī ḷi e ai o au ṃ ḥ k kh g gh ṅ ch chh j jh ñ ṭ ṭh ḍ ḍh ṇ t th d dh n p ph b bh m y r l v ś sh s h

अ A

अजपजप **ajapajapa** The holy name (*mantram*) repeating itself in the consciousness of the devotee without effort on his part.

अद्वैत **advaita** [*a* not; *dva* two] Non-dualism, the teaching which declares that all existence is One (its most eminent expounder being *Śaṃkara*).

अनाहतचक्र **anāhata-chakra** The center of consciousness (*chakra*) at the level of the heart.

अन्तःकरण **antaḥkaraṇa** [*antaḥ* inner; *karaṇa* instrument] Internal instrument, the mind.

अन्नमयकोश **annamaya-kośa** [*anna* food; *maya* made of; *kośa* sheath: "sheath made of food"] See *kośa.*

अपर **apara** [opposite of *para*] Lower knowledge, worldly knowledge.

अभय **abhaya** Fearlessness, security.

अभ्यास **abhyāsa** Regular practice, discipline.

अर्जुन **Arjuna** Name of one of the five *Pāṇḍava* brothers. He plays a major role in the epic, the *Mahābhārata,* and is the companion and disciple of *Kṛishṇa* in the *Bhagavad-Gītā.*

अर्धनारीश्वर **Ardhanārīśvara** "The Lord who is half female (and half male)," name of a form of *Śiva.*

अवतार **avatāra** [*ava-tṛī* to descend] The descent of God to earth, the incarnation of God on earth.

अविद्या **avidyā** Ignorance, spiritual blindness, illusion.

अव्यक्त **avyakta** The unmanifest.

अशोक **Aśoka** "He who has gone beyond sorrow," name of a Buddhist king in ancient India who became famous for his non-violent rule and his devotion to Buddhism.

अष्टाङ्गयोग **ashṭāṅgayoga** [*ashṭa* eight; *aṅga* limb; *yoga* discipline, path, method] "The eight-fold path," the method described by *Patañjali* in the *Yogasūtras*. The eight steps on the path are *yama, niyama, āsana, prāṇāyāma, pratyāhāra, dhāraṇa, dhyāna, samādhi* (qq. vv.).

अहंकार **ahaṃkāra** [*aham* I; *kāra* maker] Self-will, the ego mask, the principle in man which makes him feel separate from others.

अहिंसा **ahiṃsā** Non-injury, non-violence implying an attitude of love for all creatures.

आ Ā

आगामिकर्म **āgāmi-karma** Actions which have not yet been performed and their results.

आज्ञाचक्र **ājñā-chakra** "Command center," the center of consciousness (*chakra*) between the eyebrows, also referred to as the third eye.

आत्मन् **Ātman** The Self, the seed of perfection hidden within all creatures; essence.

आनन्द **ānanda** Joy, bliss.

आनन्दमयकोश **ānandamaya-kośa** [*ānanda* joy; *maya* made of; *kośa* sheath: "sheath of joy"] See *kośa.*

आरम्भशूर **ārambhaśūra** He who is a hero in the beginning (that is, one who fails to finish heroically).

आश्रम **āśrama** The home of a person or group of people who lead the spiritual life – generally the home of a spiritual teacher and his students. Ideally, it should be a quiet place which is suitable for the practice of meditation and other spiritual disciplines. In ancient India they were often located in forests or in the mountains. Even today these spiritual retreats may be found all over India.

आसन **āsana** A particular posture or way of sitting – this may refer to the posture suitable for meditation or to certain exercises practiced to promote health (third step in *Patañjali's yoga*).

इ I

इडा **iḍā** A channel or nerve which runs up the spinal column to the left of the central channel called *sushumnā.*

इन्द्रिय **indriya** An organ of sense or action.

इष्टदेवता **ishṭadevatā** A chosen diety or ideal, one particularly worshipped or followed.

ई Ī

ईश्वर **Īśvara** [*īś* to rule] The Lord; the Inner Ruler.

उ U

उपनिषद् **Upanishad** "The sitting down at the feet of a teacher to listen to his words," name of a class of mystical writings which form a part of the *Vedas*.

ऋ Ṛ I

ऋषि **ṛishi** Inspired sage, seer.

ए E

एकाग्रता **ekāgratā** One-pointedness, doing only one thing at a time, concentrating upon a single object or task.

ओ O

ओम् औम् **om** or **aum** A sacred syllable. It is uttered at the beginning and end of prayers, and is also used in the repetition of a holy name (*mantram*).

क K

कर्म **karma** [*kṛi* to do] Action; former actions which will lead to certain results in a cause and effect relationship.

कर्मयोग **karma-yoga** The path of selfless action.

काम **kāma** Desire, selfish desire, sensory craving. Name of the god of worldly love.

कामिनीकाञ्चन **kāminīkāñchana** Lust and gold.

काल **kāla** Time, death.

कालिदास **Kālidāsa** "Servant of *Kālī,*" name of a celebrated poet of ancient India, the author of *Śakuntalā, Meghadūta, Kumārasambhava* and many other famous dramas and poems.

कालिय **Kāliya** Name of a serpent-demon who is a symbol for lust and who was conquered by *Kṛishṇa.*

काली **Kālī** "The dark one," name of the Divine Mother as the consort of *Śiva.*

कुण्डलिनी **kuṇḍalinī** "The coiled-power," a force which ordinarily rests at the base of the spine, described as being coiled there like a serpent. The practice of meditation may arouse this latent power and cause it to rise up through the *sushumnā* canal which is located within the spinal column. As *kuṇḍalinī* rises the meditator begins to experience higher levels of consciousness. This unfolding of consciousness is often described in terms of the centers of consciousness (*chakras*) which are located along the *sushumnā*; as *kuṇḍalinī* rises the *chakras* are activated. *Kuṇḍalinī* completes its journey when it reaches the center of consciousness located at the top of the head (*sahasrāra*).

कुमार **kumāra** Son; prince. Name of a son of *Śiva* and *Pārvatī* who leads *Śiva's* forces against evil (he is also called *Kārttikeya* or *Skanda*).

कुरुक्षेत्र **Kurukshetra** "The Field of the *Kurus*," name of the field where the battle described in the

Bhagavad-Gītā takes place. The mystics interpret it as the battlefield within man himself, rather than as a particular geographic location.

कृपासागर **Kṛipāsāgara** [*kṛipā* grace, mercy; *sāgara* ocean] "He who is an ocean of mercy," name of *Kṛishṇa.*

कृष्ण **Kṛishṇa** [black; or from *kṛish* to draw, to attract to one's self] "The Dark One" or "He who draws us to Himself," name of an incarnation of *Vishṇu*. He was born in response to Mother Earth's plea to *Vishṇu* to save her from the evils threatening her. Many stories are told of his childhood passed in a small, simple village, and he is often worshipped in the form of a child. As a young man he was adored by all the village girls, especially *Rādhā*, and their romance symbolizes the lover-Beloved relationship which the devotee may have with the Lord. Later on he became the friend and advisor of the *Pāṇḍava* brothers, especially *Arjuna*, to whom he reveals the teachings of the *Bhagavad-Gītā.*

केशव **Keśava** "He who has long or beautiful hair," name of *Kṛishṇa.*

कोश **kośa** Sheath. There are five of these sheaths which cover the *Ātman* in man: *annamaya-kośa* "the sheath made of food" (the physical body), *prāṇamaya-kośa* "vital sheath," *mano-maya-kośa* "mental or emotional sheath," *vijñānamaya-kośa* "intellectual sheath," and *ānandamaya-kośa* "sheath of joy." These sheaths are transcended one by one as meditation deepens until the *Ātman* is revealed.

कैलास **Kailāsa** Name of a mountain, the mythical home of *Śiva*, placed in the *Himālayas* north of *Mānasa* lake.

कैलासवासिन् **Kailāsavāsin** "Dwelling on Mt. *Kailāsa*," name of *Śiva*.

क्रोध **krodha** [*krudh* to be angry] Anger.

ग G

गङ्गा **Gaṅgā** River Ganges.

गणेश **Gaṇeśa** Name of a son of *Śiva* and *Pārvatī*. He has the form of an elephant and is described as "he who removes all obstacles." He is the personification of the power and strength of God.

गीता **Gītā** See *Bhagavad-Gītā*.

गुण **guṇa** Quality; good quality. A basic quality of the world's material support (*prakṛiti*). There are three such basic qualities: *sattva* law or virtue, *rajas* passion or energy, and *tamas* ignorance or inertia. The phenomenal world is made up of a combination of these three qualities.

गुप्त **gupta** "The hidden one," name of *Kṛishṇa*.

गुरु **guru** Heavy; "He who is unshakable," a spiritual teacher.

गोपाल **gopāla** Cowherd, name of *Kṛishṇa*.

गोपी **gopī** Cowherdess, milkmaid, especially the companions of *Kṛishṇa* as a young man in *Vṛindāvana*.

गोविन्द **Govinda** Name of *Kṛishṇa*.

च CH

चक्र **chakra** "Wheel," name of the seven centers of consciousness which are described as being strung along the spine within the *sushumnā* canal. Ordinarily the force called *kuṇḍalinī* (q.v.) circulates between the three lowest *chakras*–*mulādhāra* (at the base of the spine), *svādhishṭhāna* (genital), and *maṇipūraka* (at the level of the navel) – which represent elimination, reproduction and consumption. As *kuṇḍalinī* is made to rise by the practice of spiritual disciplines it activates *anāhata* (heart center), then *viśuddhi* (throat center), then *ājñā* (between the eyebrows). Last of all the center at the top of the head called *sahasrāra* is reached.

चन्द्रशेखर **Chandraśekhara** [*chandra* moon; *śekhara* diadem] "He who has the moon as his diadem," name of *Śiva.*

चित्त **chitta** Mind-stuff.

चित्तवृत्ति **chittavṛitti** Thought-waves, activity of the mind.

चित्तवृत्तिनिरोध **chitta-vṛitti-nirodha** Control or cessation of thought-waves (this is the definition of *Yoga* given by *Patañjali*).

चित्रगुप्त **Chitragupta** Name of the recorder of every man's good and evil deeds, the "hidden auditor" who lives in every cell of our being.

ज J

जगत् **jagat** [an intensive form of *gam* to go] "That which is always going," the phenomenal world.

जपम् **japam** Repetition of a spiritual formula or holy name (*mantram*). The repetition may be either aloud or silently to one's self.

जाग्रत् **jāgrat** Waking state of consciousness.

ज्ञान **jñāna** [*jñā* to know] Wisdom, higher knowledge derived from spiritual disciplines.

ज्ञानयोग **jñāna-yoga** The path of wisdom.

त T

तत् **Tat** That – the Impersonal Supreme Reality.

तत्त्वमसि **Tat tvam asi** "That thou art." This is quoted from the deeply significant verse in the *Chhāndogya Upanishad:*

> That subtle essence which is the Self
> of this entire world, That is the Real,
> That is the Self, That thou art. (6.8.7)

तपस् **tapas** [*tap* to be hot, to shine; to make hot] Warmth, energy; undergoing self-disciplines in order to progress on the spiritual path; the power produced by such spiritual disciplines.

तमस् **tamas** Darkness, ignorance, inertia—the lowest of the three *guṇas* (q.v.).

तुरीय **turīya** "The Fourth," the highest level of consciousness, union with *Brahman*. (The other three states are waking, dreaming and dreamless sleep).

नत्यक्तेनभुञ्जीथाः **tena tyaktena bhuñjīthāḥ** (from the *Īśa Upanishad*) Renounce and enjoy.

त्याग **tyāga** [*tyaj* to renounce] Renunciation.

त्यागिन् **tyāgin** [*tyaj* to renounce] One who renounces selfish desires, self-will or the ego.

त्रिपुरान्तक **Tripurāntaka** "Destroyer of the three cities (of anger, fear and lust)," name of *Śiva.*

द D

दर्शन **darśana** [*dṛiś* to see] Seeing; audience (especially with a spiritual person); a philosophical system (six are usually listed as traditional: *Mīmāṃsā, Vedānta, Nyāya, Vaiśeshika, Sāṃkhya* and *Yoga*).

दुःख **duḥkha** Pain, suffering, sorrow.

देव **deva** [*div* to shine] "The shining one," a divine being, a god.

द्वेष **dvesha** Hatred, aversion.

ध DH

धर्म **dharma** [*dhṛi* to support] That which is established; law; duty; justice; virtue; the nature or essential quality or peculiar condition of anything; that which supports.

धर्मशाला **dharmaśālā** A resting place for pilgrims.

धारण **dhāraṇa** [*dhṛi* to hold firm] Concentration. The first stage of meditation during which the senses are gradually brought under control as concentration deepens. At the end of this stage the senses close down and physical consciousness is transcended. The meditator makes the experiential discovery that he is not the body (the sixth step in *Patañjali's yoga*).

ध्यान **dhyāna** [*dhyai* to meditate] Unbroken concentration, contemplation. The second stage of meditation during which the mind is gradually brought under control. The mind is transcended and the meditator realizes experientially that he is not the mind, but that the mind is the internal instrument, just as the body is the external instrument (the seventh step in *Patañjali's yoga*).

न N

नचिकेत **Nachiketa** Name of the young boy who receives the teaching of *Yama* in the *Kaṭha Upanishad.*

नटराज **Naṭarāja** "Lord of dance," name of *Śiva* depicted as dancing with joy upon the ego (represented by the demon *Apasmāra* "he who makes us forget who we really are").

नाम **nāma** Name; merely the name (as opposed to the reality).

नामरूप **nāmarūpa** Name and form.

नारद **Nārada** The divine sage who is a devotee of *Kṛishṇa.*

नित्य **nitya** Eternal, unchanging.

नियम **niyama** The cultivation of positive virtues such as purity and devotion to God (second step in *Patañjali's yoga*).

निर्वाण **nirvāṇa** [*nir* out; *vāṇa* blow] Extinction of self-will, Self Realization.

निर्विकल्पसमाधि **nirvikalpa-samādhi** [*nirvikalpa* having no separateness] *Samādhi* (q.v.) in which the duality of subject and object is completely transcended. There is no knower or Known, no lover or Beloved, and one experiences union with *Brahman.*

निशाचर **niśāchara** "One who moves about by night," a demon, one who uses the night for wrong purposes.

नीलकण्ठ **Nīlakaṇṭha** "Blue-throated One," name of *Śiva.*

प P

पतञ्जलि **Patañjali** The author of the *Yogasūtras* – a concise but complete description of the way to attain Self Realization through meditation. He is not the originator of the system, but has formulated it with deep insight and in a scientific manner. He probably lived around 200 B.C. The path he describes is often referred to as *ashṭāñgayoga* (q.v.).

पद्म **padma** Lotus, another name given to the centers of consciousness (*chakras*) because they are often described as containing lotuses.

पर **para** [opposite of *apara*] Transcendental, supreme; spiritual wisdom (as opposed to worldly knowledge).

पशुपति **Paśupati** "Lord of creatures," name of *Śiva.*

पार्वती **Pārvatī** "Daughter of the mountain," name of *Śiva's* wife (*śakti*) in the form of a beautiful young woman.

पिङ्गला **piñgalā** The channel or nerve which runs up the spine to the right of the central channel called *sushumnā.*

पुराण **Purāṇa** "Ancient," the name given to a class of Sanskrit scriptures, composed in verse, which relate many stories about the ancient sages and about the gods, *Brahmā, Vishṇu* and *Śiva* (these three being thought of as three manifestations of the One Absolute). These stories convey spiritual truths in a popular, vivid manner.

पुरुष **purusha** Man, the Spirit within man, the Universal Spirit.

पूजा **pūjā** Honor, worship, worship in the form of a ritual.

प्रकृति **prakṛiti** "Making before or at first," primary substance, the origin and support of the material world. It has three qualities (*guṇas*): *sattva* law, *rajas* energy, and *tamas* inertia.

प्रज्ञा **prajñā** True or transcendental wisdom, a higher mode of knowing.

प्रत्याहार **pratyāhāra** Discriminating restraint of the senses from sense objects, reconditioning the the nervous system to go beyond pleasure and pain (the fifth step in *Patañjali's yoga*).

प्रदक्षिण **pradakshiṇa** Walking around a temple or image clockwise as a form of worship.

प्रसाद **prasāda** Peace, tranquility; grace; the offering of food, etc. given to an image in worship.

प्राण **prāṇa** Breath of life, vital energy, capacity to desire and love.

प्राणमयकोश **prāṇamaya-kośa** [*prāṇa* vital energy; *maya* made of; *kośa* sheath: "vital sheath"] See *kośa.*

प्राणायाम **prāṇāyāma** Control of the vital energy and of one's desires, regulation of the breathing rhythm (fourth step in *Patañjali's yoga*).

प्रारब्धकर्म **prārabdha-karma** Results of past actions which are producing fruit in the present.

प्रेय **preya** (opposite of *śreya*) That which seems pleasing to the senses, passing pleasure.

ब B

बहिष्करण **bahishkaraṇa** [*bahish* external; *karaṇa* instrument] External instrument, the body.

बुद्ध **Buddha** [*budh* to wake up, to understand] "The awakened one," "the enlightened one," name of an illumined man born in 560 B.C. in North India whose family name was *Gautama.* After attaining enlightenment he traveled over northern India teaching the people the way to *nirvāṇa*.

बुद्धि **buddhi** [*budh* to awake, to understand] Discriminative faculty; wisdom; mental attitude; understanding.

ब्रह्मचर्य **brahmacharya** Conduct worthy of one who seeks to know *Brahman;* continence.

ब्रह्मन् **Brahman** Total Godhead, the Divine Ground of existence, the impersonal Supreme Reality.

ब्रह्मा **Brahmā** God the Creator.

भ BH

भक्त **bhakta** [*bhaj* to serve, worship, love] Devotee.

भक्ति **bhakti** [*bhaj* to serve, worship, love] Devotion, worship, love.

भक्तियोग **bhakti-yoga** The path of love and devotion.

भगवत् **Bhagavat** "The divine or adorable one," name of *Kṛishṇa.*

भगवद्गीता **Bhagavad-Gītā** "The Song of the Lord," name of a mystical poem found in the *Mahābhārata.* It is a dialogue between Lord *Kṛishṇa* and *Arjuna. Arjuna,* representing man, asks *Kṛishṇa* many searching questions and receives answers which are eloquent and direct. *Kṛishṇa* points out three paths to Self Realization: *karma-yoga* the path of selfless action, *jñāna-yoga* the path of wisdom, and *bhakti-yoga* the way of love.

भय **bhaya** Fear.

भाव **bhāva** Emotion, a way of thinking or feeling. A personal relationship with God of which there are five: *vātsalya* parent to Child, *mādhurya* lover to Beloved, *sakhya* friend to Friend, *dāsya* servant to Master, and *śānta* unitive state.

भोग **bhoga** Enjoyment of sense pleasures.

म M

मणिपूरकचक्र **maṇipūraka-chakra** The center of consciousness (*chakra*) at the level of the navel.

मदन **madana** "He who makes you mad," passion, lust; name of the god of worldly love.

मनोमयकोश **manomaya-kośa** [*manas* mind; *maya* made of; *kośa* sheath: "mental sheath"] See *kośa.*

मन्त्रम् **mantram** A spiritual formula or holy name which is inherently connected with the reality it represents.

महर्षि **maharshi** [*maha* great; *ṛishi* sage] A great sage.

महात्म **mahātma** Great soul.

महादेव **Mahādeva** "The great God," name of *Śiva.*

महाभारत **Mahābhārata** Name of the great epic composed from 2,000 to 3,000 years ago, traditionally attributed to the sage *Vyāsa.* It relates the conflict between the descendants of *Pāṇḍu* (the forces of light) and those of *Dhṛitarāshtra* (the forces of darkness).

माया **māyā** Illusion, the cosmic illusion of duality, appearance (as opposed to Reality). *Māyā* is said to have two functions: *āvaraṇa* "covering" and *vikshepa* "throwing out." The first hides the Inner Reality from us, and the second deceives us into believing that fulfillment lies without.

मार्कण्डेय **Mārkaṇḍeya** Name of a boy in the Hindu Scriptures who overcomes death through the grace of *Śiva.*

मुनि **muni** A sage.

मुमुक्षु **mumukshu** One who desires final liberation (*moksha*).

मूलाधारचक्र **mūlādhāra-chakra** The lowest center of consciousness (*chakra*) called "basal" and located at the base of the spine.

मृत्युञ्जय **Mṛityuñjaya** "The conqueror of death," name of *Śiva.*

मोक्ष **moksha** Liberation from the cycle of birth and death, complete freedom, salvation.

य Y

यम **yama** Self-control; refraining from actions, words and thoughts which harm others and which are selfish (the first step in *Patañjali's yoga*).

यम **Yama** Name of the King of Death.

याज्ञवल्क्य **Yājñavalkya** Name of the householder sage in the *Bṛihadāraṇyaka Upanishad.*

युग **yuga** An age, eon. There are four *yugas*: *Kṛita, Tretā, Dvāpara* and *Kali.* There is a steady deterioration in the state of the world from age to age. We are now living in *Kaliyuga.*

योग **yoga** [*yuj* to unite] Union, spiritual union; a method of attaining union with the Lord, a path to Self Realization; sometimes used as a proper noun to refer to the method of meditation and the philosophy taught by *Patañjali.*

र R

रजस् **rajas** Passion, desire, energy – the second of the three *guṇas* (q.v.).

राग **rāga** [*rañj* to be excited; to be attracted by] Passion, lust.

राजयोग **rājayoga** [*rāja* royal; *yoga* path: "the royal path"] The *yoga* of meditation (which combines meditation with elements of love, wisdom and service).

राधा **Rādhā** Name of *Kṛishṇa's* beloved. Their romance symbolizes the lover-Beloved relationship between the human soul and God. After experiencing the anguish of separation, *Rādhā* can be reunited with *Kṛishṇa* only when she completely surrenders herself to him in love.

राम **Rāma** [*ram* to rejoice] "He who grants abiding joy," name of an incarnation of *Vishṇu;* the principle of Joy within.

रामराज्य **Rāmarājya** The rule of *Rāma.*

रामायण **Rāmāyaṇa** The great epic poem composed by the sage *Vālmīki*. It relates the story of *Rāma* (an incarnation of *Vishṇu*) and his wife *Sītā*, and their victory over the demon king *Rāvaṇa*. *Rāma* is considered to be the ideal for men, and *Sītā* the ideal for women. Perhaps the greatest appeal of this work is its moving portrayal of the selfless devotion between husband and wife.

रावण **Rāvaṇa** The demon king who is conquered by *Rāma*. He may be regarded as the personification of self-will (*ahaṃkāra*).

रूप **rūpa** Any outward appearance or form; beauty; image.

रोग **roga** Disease.

ल L

लीला **līlā** The Divine Play of the Lord.

व V

वामन **vāmana** Dwarf, name of the fifth incarnation of *Vishṇu.*

विघ्नेश्वर **Vighneśvara** [*vighna* obstacle; *īśvara* lord] "The remover of obstacles," name of *Gaṇeśa.*

विज्ञानमयकोश **vijñānamaya-kośa** [*vijñāna* intellect; *maya* made of; *kośa* sheath: "intellectual sheath"] See *kośa.*

विभूति **vibhūti** A super-normal power (such as precognition).

विवेक **viveka** Discrimination; judgement; the ability to distinguish the Real from the unreal, the True from the false.

विशुद्धिचक्र **viśuddhi-chakra** "The center of purity," the center of consciousness (*chakra*) located near the throat.

विश्वनाथ **Viśvanātha** [*viśva* universe; *nātha* Lord] "Lord of the universe," name of *Śiva.*

विष्णु **Vishṇu** "The all-pervading one," name of one of the gods of the Hindu Trinity. He is the Preserver and descends to earth in the form of a divine incarnation when the world especially needs His grace. He is mainly worshipped in the form of his incarnations *Rāma* and *Kṛishṇa.* Altogether he has ten incarnations: the fish, tortoise, boar, man-lion, dwarf, *Paraśu-Rāma, Rāma, Kṛishṇa, Buddha* and *Kalki.*

वृन्दावन **Vṛindāvana** Name of a village on the *Jumnā* River where the historic *Kṛishṇa* spent his youth as a cowherd, befriending the local cowherds and milkmaids. Today it is an important place of pilgrimage.

वेद् **Veda** [*vid* to know] "Knowledge," the name of the most ancient Sanskrit scriptures. Orthodox Hindus regard them as the direct revelation of spiritual truth from God to the ancient sages.

वेदान्त **vedānta** [*veda* knowledge; name of the ancient Sanskrit scriptures; *anta* end: "end of the *Vedas*"] Name of one of the six philosophical traditions in India. It is called *Vedānta* because it teaches the essence of the *Vedas* and because it is founded upon the *Upanishads*, which come at the end of the *Veda*. The most eminent of its teachers is *Śaṃkara* (c. 6th or 7th century A.D.).

वैराग्य **vairāgya** Freedom from all selfish desires, detachment.

श Ś

शंकर **Śaṃkara** "Bringing about eternal welfare," name of *Śiva*. Name of the great Hindu saint of the 6th or 7th century, born in Kerala, who is the author of many philosophical works and devotional hymns. He is the leading teacher of the doctrine of non-dualism (*advaita-vedānta*).

शक्ति **śakti** Power, energy. The active power of a diety, often personified as his wife. Some of the names of the *śakti* of *Śiva* are *Durgā, Gaurī, Umā, Kālī;* of *Vishṇu* there are *Lakshmī* and *Sarasvatī.*

शब्द **śabda** Sound; a word; The Word – the syllable *OM.*

शान्ति **śānti** Tranquility, perfect peace, calmness of mind (often repeated three times at the end of a prayer as a benediction).

शिव **Śiva** ["In whom all things lie"; or "The Auspicious One"] God in the aspect of the "destroyer" who brings about the destruction of the ego (*ahaṃkāra*) and of death itself. He is usually represented as having the Ganges running through his matted locks; having snakes (which are a symbol of vital energy) around his limbs; wearing a tiger skin (having slain the tiger of lust); having a third eye (symbol of spiritual wisdom) in his forehead; and having a blue throat caused by the poison which he drank in order to save the world. He is one of the Hindu Trinity, the others being *Vishṇu* and *Brahmā*.

शिष्य **śishya** [*śās* to teach] "One who is to be taught," a disciple, student.

श्रद्धा **śraddhā** Faith, belief.

श्रेय **śreya** (opposite of *preya*) The Good, that which leads to lasting welfare.

स S

संयम **saṃyama** The three stages of meditation – *Dhāraṇa, Dhyāna* and *Samādhi* (especially when they are practiced upon a particular idea or object).

संसार **saṃsāra** [*sṛi* to move] The cycle of birth and death, the flux of life.

संस्कार **saṃskāra** A deep mental impression produced by past experiences, a mental or behavioral pattern, a latency.

संस्कृत **saṃskṛita** Polished, perfected; name of the language of the ancient Hindus.

सङ्कल्प **sañkalpa** Mental activity (especially will or desire).

सञ्चितकर्म **sañchita-karma** Results of past actions which have not yet become manifest.

सच्चिदानन्द **Sat-Chit-Ānanda** Absolute Existence-Absolute Knowledge-Absolute Bliss.

सत्यंशिवंसुन्दरं **Sattyam Śivam Sundaram** Truth-Bliss-Beauty.

सत्य **satya** Truth, reality.

सत्त्व **sattva** Law, reality, purity – the highest of the three *guṇas* (q.v.).

सत्सङ्ग **satsaṅga** Association with spiritually oriented people.

समाधि **samādhi** [*sam* with; *ādhi* Lord: "union with the Lord." Or *sam-ā-dhā* to hold or fix together, to concentrate upon] Deep concentration in which the mind becomes still and is transcended. In this state a higher mode of knowing is experienced and the duality of subject and object disappears. Union with the Lord, Self Realization. The last of the three stages of meditation (and the last step in *Patañjali's yoga*).

सरूप **sarūpa** With form, having form.

सविकल्पसमाधि **savikalpa-samādhi** [*savikalpa* having distinctions or admitting separateness] *Samādhi* (q.v.) in which some duality of subject and object remains – the devotee being absorbed in his meditation upon the Lord without becoming completely one with Him. Union with the personal God.

सहस्रार **sahasrāra** "Thousand-spoked," the center of consciousness (*chakra*) located at the top of the head. It is said to resemble a thousand-petalled lotus.

सहोदर **sahodara** [*saha* together; *udara* womb] "Born of the same womb," a brother or sister.

साधक **sādhaka** One who practices spiritual disciplines (*sādhana*).

साधन **sādhana** Body of disciplines which lead to Self Realization.

साधु **sādhu** A holy man, sage.

सिद्धार्थ **Siddhārtha** "He who has fulfilled his purpose," name of *Gautama* the *Buddha*.

सिद्धि **siddhi** A super-normal power (such as precognition).

सीता **Sītā** Name of the wife of *Rāma*. She is considered to be the ideal for women.

सुख **sukha** Pleasure, that which is pleasing to the senses, mind and ego.

सुषुप्ति **sushupti** Dreamless sleep.

सुषुम्ना **sushumnā** A channel in the center of the spinal column in which are located the seven centers of consciousness (*chakras*) and through which the force called *kuṇḍalinī* (coiled-power) rises.

सूक्ष्मशरीर **sūkshma-śarīra** [*sūkshma* subtle; *śarīra* body] The subtle body which is not destroyed at the death of the physical body and which accompanies the soul in its transmigration. It is essentially composed of the mental characteristics (*saṃskāras*) of the individual.

सूत्र **sūtra** Thread; an aphorism or short sentence (upon which the thoughts of the author are hung as beads on a string); a book composed of such aphorisms.

स्थितप्रज्ञ **sthitaprajña** [*sthita* established; *prajñā* spiritual wisdom] One who is established in spiritual wisdom.

स्थूलशरीर **sthūla-śarīra** [*sthūla* gross; *śarīra* body] The physical body.

स्फोट **sphoṭa** Sound, vibration, The Word. According to the theory of vibrations this is the subtle stuff out of which the phenomenal world has emanated.

स्वधर्म **svadharma** One's own *dharma* (q.v.), the law of one's being.

स्वप्न **svapna** Dream state of consciousness.

स्वाधिष्ठानचक्र **svādhishṭhāna-chakra** The center of consciousness (*chakra*) at the level of the genitals.

ह H

हंस **haṃsa** Swan, a symbol for the Supreme Reality. The *Haṃsa* is said to have the *mantram so'ham ahaṃ saḥ* "I am He, He is me." Those who have attained spiritual awareness are sometimes called *Paramahaṃsa* "the Great Swan."

हनुमान् **Hanumān** Name of the monkey devotee of *Rāma.*

हरि **Hari** [*hṛi* to steal] "He who has stolen our hearts," name of *Vishṇu* or *Kṛishṇa.*

हिमालय **Himālaya** "The abode of snow," name of the great range of mountains which bounds India on the north. It has always been the home of many spiritual retreats and places of pilgrimage.

हृषीकेश **Hṛishīkeśa** [*hṛishī* ecstatic; *keśa* hair. Or *hṛishīka* senses; *īśa* Lord] "He whose hair stands on end in ecstasy" or "Lord of the senses," name of *Kṛishṇa.*